1,000,000 Books

are available to read at

---

www.ForgottenBooks.com

Read online
Download PDF
Purchase in print

ISBN 978-0-332-49068-7
PIBN 11235029

English
Français
Deutsche
Italiano
Español
Português

www.forgottenbooks.com

Mythology Photography **Fiction**
Fishing Christianity **Art** Cooking
Essays Buddhism Freemasonry
Medicine **Biology** Music **Ancient**
Egypt Evolution Carpentry Physics
Dance Geology **Mathematics** Fitness
Shakespeare **Folklore** Yoga Marketing
Confidence Immortality Biographies
Poetry **Psychology** Witchcraft
Electronics Chemistry History **Law**
Accounting **Philosophy** Anthropology
Alchemy Drama Quantum Mechanics
Atheism Sexual Health **Ancient History**
Entrepreneurship Languages Sport
Paleontology Needlework Islam
Metaphysics Investment Archaeology
Parenting Statistics Criminology
Motivational

SEVENTY-SEVENTH ANNUAL REPORT

of the

Montana State Board of Dental Examiners

To His Excellency
GOVERNOR FORREST H. ANDERSON

1970

PERSONNEL

MONTANA STATE BOARD OF DENTAL EXAMINERS

Dr. James C. Moses, Wolf Point..President

Dr. Dean P. Sullivan, Sr, Billings ....Vice-President

Dr. Dean D. Koffler, Lewistown...Secretary-Treasurer

Dr. James E. Smith, Livingston .... Member

Dr. Edgar J. Guay, Butte... Member

✖   ✖   ✖

BOND

The Secretary-Treasurer of the Montana State Board of Dental Examiners is covered by a blanket bond covering all state officers and employees. This bond was purchased by the State Controller.

✖   ✖   ✖

Although care has been exercised in compiling this directory, no responsibility is assumed for errors or omissions. Your co-operation in directing our attention to possible corrections will be appreciated.

PROCEEDINGS

To: His Excellency, Forrest Anderson
Governor of the State of Montana
Helena, Montana

SEVENTY-SEVENTH REGULAR MEETING
Montana State Board of Dental Examiners
Billings, Montana, July 12, 1970

The meeting was called to order at 1:00 P.M. by Dr. Smith, President. All Board members were in attendance. Representatives of both Dental Supply houses were present to discuss setting up of facilities and arranging schedules to best accommodate patients and candidates. This was necessary because of the larger than usual number of candidates taking the Board. Both representatives left following this discussion.

The following items of business were discussed or acted upon:

1. Dr. Koffler, Secretary, presented a bill from Worden, Worden, Robb and Thane of Missoula in the amount of $953.33 for legal services rendered on behalf of the Board in Missoula. Dr. Koffler informed the Board that the Montana State Dental Association has been asked to share this cost and their final decision will be made at the regular meeting, January, 1971.

2. The following licenses were revoked for default of payment of annual license fee after 30 days had passed since notification by certified letter: Dr. W. M. Smith, South Gate, Calif.; Dr. Kenneth Severn, Fergus Falls, Minn.; Dr. Charles Padbury, Portland, Ore.; Dr. L. F. Inman, Billings, Mont.; and Dental Hygienist Doteen Baker (Mundy), Beaverton, Ore.

3. It was decided by the Board that at this time evidence of continuing education need not be presented to retain a dental license but that the present policy of giving credit for attending educational programs should be continued.

MEETING ADJOURNED UNTIL 9:00 A.M., THURSDAY, JULY 16.

4. The Secretary was instructed to check with officials at Malmstrom AFB to determine the feasibility of holding the annual dental examination there in 1971. A report to the Board is to be made at the January, 1971 meeting or before.

5. The annual meeting of the National Association of Dental Examiners will be held in Las Vegas, Nevada, Nov. 5-6, 1970. Dr. Guay will represent the Montana Board.

6. After much discussion concerning the use of auxiliary personnel, the Board decided not to specify duties but to refer to the specifications as covered in the Dental Practice Act.

Officers elected for the coming year were Dr. J. C. Moses, Wolf Point, President; Dr. D. P. Sullivan, Billings, Vice-President; Dr. D. D. Koffler, Lewistown, Secretary-Treasurer.

President Smith adjourned the meeting at 2:20 P.M.

Respectfully submitted,

Dean D. Koffler, D.D.S.
Secretary-Treasurer
Montana State Board of Dental Examiners

Licenses to practice dentistry in the State of Montana were granted to:

Barbian, Dennis H. .... 642 Plymouth Ave., Missoula, Mont. 59801

Barrow, Bruce L. .... Box 1096, Crow Agency, Mont. 59022

Blevins, Donald **E.** .... 1610 Morgan St., Keokuk, Iowa 52632

Bluher, John A. .... Cody Medical Center, Cody, Wyo. 82414

Capener, Daryl M. .... 1028 E. Walnut Crk. Pkwy., West Covina, Calif. 91790

Congdon, William J. .... Box 361, Sandstone, Minn. 55072

Eickman, Tim H. .... 709 California St., Libby, Mont. 59923

Fry, Robert M. .... 1229 N. 25th St, . Billings, Mont. 59101

Johnson, James H. .... 1739 Grand Ave, Billings, Mont. 59102

Kastrop, Marvin C. .... 915 Avenue F, Billings, Mont. 59102

Magnuson, Jay W. .... Rt. 1, Box 155, White Swan, Wash. 98952

McDonald, C. J. .... 2314 Buena Vista, Walnut Creek, Calif. 94596

Mihelish, Gary L. .... Box 356, Lame Deer, Mont. 59043

Neil, Robin .... 3406 4th Ave., Great Falls, Mont. 59401

Nordstrom, Donald O. .... 1103 Hollywood Blvd., Iowa City, Iowa 52240

Olson, James W. .... 24 White Oak, Jacksonville, N. C. 28540

Richter, Edward A. .... 612 Louise, Ann Arbor, Mich. 48103

Schmit, Gary R. .... 2613 3rd St. Plaza So., Omaha, Neb. 68108

Schwartzenberger, Garold .... 729 W. Daly St., Walkerville, Mont. 59701

Sperry, John D. .... 1223 S. Higgins Ave., Missoula, Mont. 59801

Urban, David **E.** .... 90th Med. Detachment, APO N. Y. 09154

Wagner, Robert P. .... 1320 Fifth Ave., Prince George, B. C.

Wescott, Francis L. .... Box 266, Ainsworth, Neb. 69210

Wight, Lee M. .... 1500 E. Katell Ave., Orange, Calif. 92667

Wilson, Kent **E.** .... Ohio St. Univ. Col. of Dentistry, Columbus, Ohio 43212

Wood, Richard S. .... 4855 Cole St., San Diego, Calif. 92117

Licenses to practice dental hygiene in the State of Montana were granted to:

Becker, Lois M. .... 443 S. Gaylord, Denver, Colo. 80209

Lipp, Margaret R. .... 775 Monroe, Apt. 203, Missoula, Mont. 59801

Weibert, Elizabeth J. .... Harlem, Mont. 59526

WINTER MEETING
Billings, Montana, January 14, 1970

The meeting was called to order at 2:15 P.M. by Dr. James Smith, President. All Board members were present and the minutes from the July, 1969, meeting were approved.

The following items of business were discussed or acted upon:

1. Dr. Dean D. Koffler, new Board member and new Secretary-Treasurer, reported on present finances of the Board and projected income for 1970. The new annual license fee schedule was set as follows:

Resident Dentists $15.00

Non-residents and Dentists in Military_ $10.00

Retired Dentists who retain license .... $ 5.00

All licensed Dental Hygienists ....$ 3.00

2. The Secretary was authorized to repay the Montana State Dental Association one-half of the legal fee incurred for revising the Montana Dental Practice Act. President Smith also read correspondence concerning the practice of dentistry by non-licensed persons in District 2 dental district. Current legal action is pending.

3. A request by the State of Iowa to reciprocate with the State of Montana in the matter of honoring state dental boards was declined

4. The dates of July 13, 14, 15 were set as the official dates the annual Montana State Board Dental Examinations will be given in Billings, Montana.

5. The possibility of listing telephone numbers in the next annual report was discussed and tabled when it was decided this would not be of any special advantage to most of the membership.

6. The possibility of acquiring a permanent secretary for the Board of Dental Examiners was discussed. This may involve sharing a full-time secretary or assistant secretary with other state dental groups. It was agreed that a permanent secretary would be desirable and further research should be done concerning this possibility.

7. The Secretary was authorized to buy an inexpensive copy machine to be used by the Secretary for necessary Board work.

President Smith adjourned the meeting at 5:00 P.M.

Respectfully submitted,

Dean D. Koffler, D.D.S.
Secretary-Treasurer
Montana State Board of Dental Examiners

SPRING MEETING
Bozeman, Montana, May 6, 1970

The meeting was called to order at 2:00 P.M. by President Dr. Jim Smith. Dr. Dean Sullivan was welcomed as a new member of the Board from Billings, Montana. Dr. Hawkins, retiring member of the Board, was also present and appreciation was expressed for his dedicated service as Board member and secretary. Dr. Farnsworth and Dr. Hawkins will be presented wall plaques for past service on the Board.

The following items of business were discussed or acted upon:

1. It was decided not to send a delegate to the National Board Secretaries Conference.

2. Considerable discussion was held concerning duties of the dental assistant but no action was taken. This matter will be considered at later meetings after further study.

3. Dr. Guay was appointed to bring X-rays and models of patients to be used in the Oral Diagnosis exam to be given in July. The Board members will evaluate the material and arrive at an adequate Oral Diagnosis exam.

4. Frank Sennett, administrative assistant to Governor Anderson, met with the Board of Dental Examiners to discuss State Reorganization of Boards. This item will be on the ballot in the November election. Mr. Sennett stated that the proposals have been revised and will probably be re-revised before the final proposal is sent out to all Boards for their consideration. He stated that even though the proposal fails on the November ballot reorganization will still proceed, but not under mandate as will be the case if it is successful. Hopefully, reorganization will create more coordination in State Government. The uniqueness of the Dental profession will probably require that Dentists continue to give the practical Dental examination.

5. Dr. Koffler reported on the progress of applicants for license information. He also advised the Board members that a $1,775.00 budget correction was necessary to complete the fiscal year.

6. Dr. Koffler presented a revised information sheet for Board examinees which was revised and printed after the January meeting. This was necessary because of changes made in the Dental Practice Act.

7. The Secretary of the American Association of Dental Examiners, B. J. Crawford, contacted Montana Board Secretary Dr. Dean Koffler and requested we reconsider and conduct the Second Cycle Survey of Montana licensed dentists which was previously requested by his office but declined by our Board. Dr. Koffler agreed to conducting this Survey after contacting members of the Montana Board of Dental Examiners and receiving a pledge of office assistance in mailing and tabulating from Mr. Crawford. The Survey is well under way and should be completed about July 1, 1970.

8. In August of 1968 representatives of the Second District Dental Society and State Board of Dental Examiners Delegate, Dr. Robert Hawkins, met with a Missoula law firm and enlisted their service to prevent a laboratory man, Mr. Hoffman, from doing dentures directly for the public. There were numerous postponements and delays by the defense lawyer and when the trial finally took place on Tuesday, Sept. 30, 1969, the jury decided he was not guilty by reason of the statute of limitations running out.

Following this decision it was decided to attempt to stop Mr. Hoffman's work by the injunction route. On Nov. 5, 1969, a complaint was filed in the Fourth Judicial District Court seeking a permanent injunction. An appearance was made by all concerned parties before Judge Green at 2:00 P.M., Nov. 20, 1969. On Feb. 17, 1970, a judgment against Mr. Hoffman, permanently enjoining him against further illegal practice of dentistry, was made.

Dr. Smith adjourned the meeting at 5:30 P.M.

Respectfully submitted,

Dean D. Koffler, D.D.S.
Secretary-Treasurer
Montana State Board of Dental Examiners

MONTANA STATE BOARD OF DENTAL EXAMINERS
SUMMARY OF CASH BALANCE
July 1, 1969, through June 30, 1970   Exhibit A

Cash on Hand—July 1, 1969.. $1,733.65
RECEIPTS:

Fees—Resident Dentists	$4,999.50	
Non-Resident Dentists	2,158.50	
Dental Hygienists	223.00	
Examinations	1,535.00	
Certificates	255.00	
Penalties	34.00	
Sale of Annual Reports	20.00	$9,225.00

Total Cash Available 10,958.65

LESS: Expenditures per Exhibit B.. 7,309.31

Cash on Hand—June 30, 1970.. $3,649.34

MONTANA STATE BOARD OF DENTAL EXAMINERS
SUMMARY OF APPROPRIATION FUND TRANSACTIONS
July 1, 1969, through June 30, 1970   Exhibit B

	Budget	Actual
Appropriations—July 1, 1969	$5,802.00	$5,802.00
Additional Appropriations	1,775.00	1,775.00
Total Appropriations	$7,577.00	$7,577.00

EXPENDITURES:

Salaries	$1,300.00	$1,193.28
Social Security	112.00	126.72
Supplies and Materials	540.00	550.42
Communication and Postage..	310.00	315.36
Travel	2,100.00	1,824.92
Contracted Services	1,530.00	1,802.65
Special Fees	1,510.00	1,198.46
Capital Expenditures	175.00	297.50
Total Expenditures	$7,577.00	$7,309.31

Fund Balance—June 30, 1970.. $ 267.69

REPORT OF THE EIGHTY-SIXTH ANNUAL MEETING OF
THE AMERICAN ASSOCIATION OF DENTAL EXAMINERS

DR. EDGAR J. GUAY, Delegate

The American Association of Dental Examiners held its annual meeting on October 9-10, 1969, in New York City.

Dr. Clifford F. Loader, President of the association, presided. In his presidential address to the General Assembly, Dr. Loader focused his attention on regional boards of dental examiners, attitudes toward dental examining boards, and relating dental change to national change.

At the symposium on Continuing Education, Dr. William R. Mann, dean, University of Michigan School of Dentistry; Guy R. Willis, member, North Carolina State Board of Dental Examiners; and Alex Parks, LL.B., former executive secretary, Oregon State Board of Dental Examiners, presented their views concerning continuing education and answered questions from the more than two hundred dental examiners, educators and members of organized dentistry who attended the symposium.

The General Assembly approved research into a character reference program to provide information on candidates for dental licensure patterned after a similar program sponsored by the National Conference of Bar Examiners.

Harry M. Bohannan, dean, University of Kentucky College of Dentistry, addressed the General Assembly and gave his impression of the Dental Curriculum for the Needs of the Future.

Newly elected officers for 1969-1970 were: Wade H. Breeland, D.D.S., president; Ray E. Stevens, D.D.S., president-elect; Donald F. Wallace, D.D.S., first vice-president; John E. Wold, D.M.D., second vice-president; Thomas C. Bradshaw, D.D.D., third vice-president.

Respectfully submitted,

E. J. Guay, D.D.S.

MONTANA DENTISTS

As of September 1, 1970

R—Retired

Abbott, Edward F...........3926 3rd Ave. S., Great Falls 59401
Akland, Richard H..............2718 3rd Ave. N., Billings 59101
Allen, Fredrik A.................228 Buffalo Block, Kalispell 59901
Allen, Michael L................Box 368, Columbia Falls 59912
Allison, William M..............505 1st Ave. E., Kalispell 59901
Andersen, Harry M.............1301 Division St., Billings 59102
Anderson, Allan M...Medical-Dental Center, Missoula 59801
Anderson, D. Dean........218 W. Broadway, Lewistown 59457
Arvish,Raymond F................413 State St., Hamilton 59840
Atchinson, John J...............P. O. Box 435, Whitefish 59937

Bailey, A. Eugene...........1304 19th St. S., Great Falls 59401
Balestra, Lawrence F...........301 N. 32nd St., Billings 59101
Barth, Donald M.........539 Kensington Ave., Missoula 59801
Bartlett, Richard N.....1824 10th Ave. S., Great Falls 59401
Bartoletti, Edward A................60 E. Broadway, Butte 59701
Bauer, Donald F....................P. O. Box 608, Superior 59872
Beagle, G. A......................120 2nd Ave. S.W., Sidney 59270
Beebe, R. Marvin............Box 137, Rte. 1, Hamilton 59840
Belhumeur, Rodolphe A.............................1125 2nd Ave. N.,
Great Falls 59401
Bell, Norman J................414 Electric Bldg., Billings 59101
Bender, John Joseph..................130 W. Galena, Butte 59701
Bessire, William B............313 Western Montana Bank Bldg.,
Missoula 59801
Betzer, Chester H................1231 N. 29th St., Billings 59101
Betzner, Robert O...307-8 Power Block Bldg., Helena 59601
Betzner, Theodore C...3990 N. Montana Ave., Helena 59601
Beveridge, Leroy................1311 11th St. W., Billings 59102
Bilden, Don R...Columbus 59019
Boifeuillet, George D.........218 E. Front St., Missoula 59801
R Bond, Eugene W.......................P. O. Box 230, Dillon 59725
Boom, Kenneth B..........P. O. Box 684, Livingston 59047
Boussard, C. P......................P.O. Box 358, Choteau 59422
Bowden, Paul H.....316-322 Miners Bank Bldg., Butte 59701
R Braaten, Albert N..................2207 Ash St., Billings 59101
Brandt, Kenneth L..........P. O. Box 568, Deer Lodge 59722
Brockway, Robert L......................401 First Natl. Bank Bldg.,
Bozeman 59715
Brown, James O., Sr................218 W. Bell, Glendive 59330
Brown, James O., Jr................218 W. Bell, Glendive 59330
Browning, Robert B.......Medical Center, Forsyth 59327
R Bucher, Charles N...............P. O. Box 593, Hamilton 59840
Bundy, Donald C.................736 S. Higgins, Missoula 59801
Burgan, D. Albert....304 Milwaukee Ave., Deer Lodge 59722
Burgan, Dwight E.....304 Milwaukee Ave., Deer Lodge 59722

Callaghan, James P...........515 Kensington, Missoula 59801
Campanella, Robert A...105 W. Callender, Livingston 59047
Carstens, Christy M.............941 Grand Ave., Billings 59102
Cerkovnik, Edward A.................P. O. Box 488, Malta 59538
Cerkovnik, Michael F...............P. O. Box 334, Sidney 59270
Chenovick, Dennis A........1093 Helena Ave., Helena 59601
Chernasek, Warren W.........P. O. Box 809, Glasgow 59230
Cherry, William E...........P. O. Box 145, Fort Benton 59442
Chinske, Edward L..Havre 59501

Christenot, Fred A...............P. O. Box 972, Livingston 59047
Christenot, Kenneth E.........P. O. Box 438, Cut Bank 59427
Cloyd, Wallace W..................P. O. Box 684, Livingston 59047
Cogley, Elmer A.............................417-418 Montana Bldg.,
Great Falls 59401
Collins, Griffith G...............Mancoronel Bldg., Conrad 59425
Constenius, John N.......427 Spokane Ave., Whitefish 59937
Cory, Clifford D...504½ Central Ave. W., Great Falls 59401
Cotner, Robert B.........P. O. Box 566, Columbia Falls 59912
Cotter, Samuel G................311 N. Broadway, Billings 59101
Crossman, Harold B...2507 6th Ave. S., Great Falls 59401
Crouch, James H...........602 Strain Bldg., Great Falls 59401
Cummerford, Charles M...11 Division Rd., Great Falls 59401
Curry, Edson M......................905 S. Main, Kalispell 59901

Dachs, George R...............795 Sunset Blvd., Kalispell 59901
Dailey, L. L........................2703 11th Ave. N., Billings 59101
Dailey, Stephen R........Professional Village, Missoula 59801
Daley, Warren L...........2503 6th Ave. S., Great Falls 59401
Danskin, Robert E.............1311 11th St. W., Billings 59102
Dean, Galen R.............219 Medical Arts Bldg., Butte 59701
Dean, Robert W.........3224 10th Ave. S., Great Falls 59401
Delaney, Douglas L..............514 Kensington, Missoula 59801
DeMille, Frederick E...28 Holiday Village, Great Falls 59401
Deutsch, Thomas J......................744 S. Main, Kaispell 59901
Devich, M. L........122 E. Commercial Ave., Anaconda 59711
Diggs, David V..................1547 S. Higgins, Missoula 59801
Doering, Gordon L.............907 Helena Ave., Helena 59601
Doering Walter B..............907 Helena Ave., Helena 59601
Dohrman, Stanley T....3016 3rd Ave. N., Great Falls 59401
Douma, Dave A................708 W. Main, Bozeman 59715
Downey, David W...........795 Sunset Blvd., Kalispell 59901
Downing, Michael H....................210 W. 2nd, Hardin 59034
Dayro, Eli W................503 Ford Bldg., Great Falls 59401
Drinkwater, George C.............336 1st Ave., Havre 59501
Durham, Leo K................204 N. 11th Ave., Bozeman 59715
Durham, Lindon C.........P. O. Box 6, Three Forks 59752

Ehrlich, M. F...............221 Medical Arts Bldg., Butte 59701
Elder, D. J.........................P. O. Box 626, Miles City 59301
Englert, Robert E.........1405 4th Ave. N., Great Falls 59401
Englund, Duane A.......1121 S. Higgins Ave., Missoula 59801
Erickson, Donald R.............1231 N. 29th St., Billings 59101
Espeland, Selmer M., Jr.........P. O. Box 788, Glasgow 59230
Evans, Earl D....................30 S. Montana St., Dillon 59725
Evans, Jerome P..................1234 Avenue C, Billings 59102
Evers, Alvin A....402 1st Natl. Bank Bldg., Bozeman 59715

Farrell, Harry G.................302 Thornton Bldg., Butte 59701
Farrell, Richard M....................Thornton Bldg., Butte 59701
R Fee, A. S..........................P. O. Box 742, Missoula 59801
Fellows, Thomas W.................208 N. 11th, Bozeman 59715
Fennessy, Thomas F.........401 Louisianna Ave., Libby 59923
Filppula, Leonard G.....17th St. W. & Ave. D, Billings 59102
Fischer, Donald F...................P. O. Box 641, Shelby 59474
Flynn, Edward J.........1125 2nd Ave. N., Great Falls 59401
French, Davy Allen.............................Box 718, Eureka 59917

Fry, Mervin R..............305 Hart-Albin Bldg., Billings 59101
Fry, William M.,................1221 S. Higgins, Missoula 59801
Fulbright, James L.........542 Central Ave., Whitefish 59937

Gallus, E. J...........................P. O. Box 517, Chinook 59523
Gallus, Raymond C............................Box 746, Havre 59501
George, Donald A.....501 Medical Arts Bldg., Butte 59701
Gilpin, John C.......................19 N. 8th St., Bozeman 59715
Gold, William H.,........14 Holiday Village, Great Falls 59401
Gorder, Clarence V.....Montana Power Bldg., Roundup 59072
Gordon, Carey H.............Rt. 1, P. O. Box 29, Polson 59860
Graham, Dwight P.............414 Great Falls Natl. Bank Bldg.,
                                                          Great Falls 59401
Granger, C. W.................................Box 55, Lakeside 59922
Gray, Charles N............................Box 387, Glasgow 59230
Greany, Byron J.................Copper Road, Anaconda 59711
Guay, Edgar J.............201 Medical Arts Bldg., Butte 59701

Hageman, Bernard ....Philipsburg 59858
Hamilton, Richard D..........1415 Grand Ave., Billings 59102
Hammer, Donald G...........P. O. Box 386, Manhattan 59741
Hand, Ronald M.......4951 B, Ave. C, Great Falls 59401
Hanna, James C..............1711 13th St. W., Billings 59102
Hansen, Kenneth R....515 Kensington Ave., Missoula 59801
Hansen, Norman M.......Gallatin Valley Med.-Dental Center,
                                                          Bozeman 59715
Hansen, Wayne L.....17th St. W. & Ave. D, Billings 59101
Hansford, Curtis S....................Box 188, Plentywood 59254
R Hawke, John C...........................409 Evans, Missoula 59801
Hawkins, Robert Allen........715 W. Central, Missoula 59801
Haynes, O. Gary......Box 786, 12 Harriet Ave., Baker 59313
Helmer M. Thomas..................1234 Ave. C, Billings 59102
Herries, J. D.................................Big Timber 59011
Herzog, Joseph A.............1250 Harrison Ave., Butte 59701
Hickman, James R.........Gallatin Valley Med.-Dental Center,
                                                          Bozeman 59715
Hogan, Richard L...................1812 Clark, Miles City 59301
Holzberger, Lloyd .F............211 Great Falls Natl. Bank Bldg.,
                                                          Great Falls 59401
Hull, G. Clayton...........................Box 43, Great Falls 59401

Ivers, Sheldon.............2501 6th Ave. S., Great Falls 59401

Jelinek, Donald P...............College Park Med.-Dental Center,
                                                          Great Falls 59401
Johnson, Archie P.....608 Montana Bldg., Lewistown 59457
Johnson, J. Donovan...........807 Grand Ave., Billings 59102
Johnson, Malcolm F.............925 Oilfield Ave., Shelby 59474
Johnson, Melvin E............415 State St., Hamilton 59840
Johnson, Richard H....................307 Medical-Dental Center,
                                                          Missoula 59801
Johnston, Edward P..........709 California Ave., Libby 59923
Jones, Enos L....................1231 N. 29th St., Billings 59101
Jones, James D..................217 W. Main, Cut Bank 59427
Jones, Llewellyn L............129 W. Kent, Missoula 59801
Jones, R. B.......................217 W. Main, Cut Bank 59427
Jones, Stephen F.....................10 S. Idaho St., Butte 59701
Jones, William J...............217 W. Main, Cut Bank 59427
Jordon, Andrew A..........................Box 757, Choteau 59422
Jourdonnais, Jon A.......2511 6th Ave. S., Great Falls 59401
Joyce, Ronald T..............1204 1st Ave. N., Kalispell 59901

Kall, John C.............................15 S. Benton, Helena 59601
Kane, J. F........................304 Thornton Bldg., Butte 59701
Kapust, John L................................Box 906, Scobey 59263
Keane, S. P...410 Power Block, 7 W. 6th Ave., Helena 59601
Kelley, R. W....................1231 N. 29th St., Billings 59101
Kemp, Robert W.................P. O. Box 408, Culbertson 59218
Kenck, Norman F.........Gallatin Valley Med.-Dental Center,
                                                          Bozeman 59715
Kennedy, John D....................College Park Medical Center,
                                                          Great Falls 59401
Kiely, Arthur W.............1820 Harrison Ave., Butte 59701
Kirby, John J.............................P. O. Box 866, Butte 59701
Kitt, Sidney P...........................108 Main, Sheridan 59747
Kluge, B. E............Room 323-4, Fratt Bldg., Billings 59101
Klunder, Bill L.............1739 Grand Ave., Billings 59102
Knight, Warren J...Florence 59833
Koffler, Dean D.................625 N.E. Main, Lewistown 59457
Kohl, Joseph G...Stevensville 55870
Karn, James H...................140 5th St. W., Kalispell 59901
Kreck, Loren L..............795 Sunset Blvd., Kalispell 59901
Kurta, John A...............P. O. Box 98, Columbia Falls 59912

Laine, Maurice D., Jr.......1547 S. Higgins, Missoula 59801
LaValley, Jerome P..........P. O. Box 631, Livingston 59047
Lawrence, Kenneth J...........1224 W. Main, Hamilton 59840
Leeds, Philip J......................P. O. Box 326, Havre 59501
Linden, C. M....................215 Ford Bldg., Great Falls 59401
Linden, Franz.....................215 Ford Bldg., Great Falls 59401
Linduska, John C...............330 S. Idaho St., Dillon 59725
Little, Thomas D.....Room 4, Whipps Bldg., Kalispell 59901
Livingstone, Neil C...........820 Montana Ave., Helena 59601
Lodmell, E. W.........................P. O. Box 1006, Polson 59860
Lahman, John W.........214 Miners Bank Bldg., Butte 59701
Lorentz, Henry B...307 Medical Arts Bldg., Butte 59701
Lynn, Everett L...................1400 8th Ave., Helena 59601

MacDonald, Alexander C...111 W. Brennan, Glendive 59930
MacDonald, Ralph F............................Medical-Dental Center,
                                                          Missoula 59801
Mackenzie, Allan S.....605 Montana Bldg., Lewistown 59457
MacPherson, Cole L...................306 Medical-Dental Center,
                                                          Missoula 59801
Madsen, John K,.....................715 Getchell, Helena 59601
Maggard, Robert P.............1106½ Main St., Billings 59101
Maixner, Marion G...................................Harlowton 59036
Malmend, Thomas I...............P. O. Box 621, Plains 59859
Manion, Robert J....................P. O. Box 327, Circle 59215
Martens, Robert L..............P. O. Box 288, Glasgow 59230
Maryott, Manfred S.................513 S. 3rd, Bridger 59014
McCollum, John B...................P. O. Box 1255, Dillon 59725
McDonald, Robert S........................Box 388, Hardin 59034
McGreevey, Franklin G............P. O. Box 566, Ronan 59864
McIntee, Leo A.... ....908 Maryland Ave., Butte 59701
McKillican, D. J.........Broadwater Hospital, Townsend 59644
McLaughlin, John H...........740 Helena Ave., Helena 59601
McPherson, David R.........P. O. Box 1308, Glendive 59330
McPherson, William E......P. O. Box 804, Chinook 59523
Meismer, Robert J......928 Broadwater Ave., Billings 59102
Messinger, Earl W..........P. O. Box 342, Plentywood 59254
Messinger, Franklin A......P. O. Box 218, Plentywood 59254
Mildenberger, James D.......P. O. Box 747, Hamilton 59840
Miller, Robert A................1711 13th St. W., Billings 59102
R Minette, C. H........................622 E. Main, Cut Bank 59427

Mitchell, John Pat........c/o Dr. Harry Farrell, Thornton Bldg.,
Butte 59701
Moline, LeRoy M..........................Box 1291, Glendive 59330
Monroe, Stephen L................Whipps Bldg., Kalispell 59901
Morris, John A..................⁚........Box 306, Whitehall 59759
R Morrow, W. D...........................P. O. Box 521, Harlem 59526
Moses, James C............217 2nd Ave. S., Wolf Point 59201
Mueske, LeRoy E...................2000 Ottawa St., Butte 59701
Murphy, Joseph J.........3511 1st Ave. N., Great Falls 59401
Murphy, Robert G.......................301 Medical-Dental Center,
Missoula 59801

Nansel, Arlo D..........................12 N. 7th, Miles City 59301
Nelson, James E.........1125 2nd Ave. N., Great Falls 59401
Nelson, Keith W.............................Box 559, Polson 59860
Netterberg, Robert E..........⁚.22 W. Front St., Butte 59701
Neubauer, Wesley C............P. O. Box 267, Glasgow 59230
Newett, B. C...............⁚.........P. O. Box 366, St. Ignatius 59865
Noonan, John T...........1121 2nd Ave. N., Great Falls 59401
Nord, Vernon A............3926 3rd Ave. S., Great Falls 59401
Norgaard, Stanley N..........218 E. Front St., Missoula 59801
Norman, Mark E.............P. O. Box 908, Conrad 59425
Nottingham, D. A...................212' 1st Ave., Laurel 59044

Olson, Fred A...................530 Kensington, Missoula 59801
Olson, M. Duane........1223 S. Higgins Ave., Missoula 59801
O'Neill, Donald James......2000 Florence Ave., Butte 59701
Orser, R. M...........................P. O. Box 942, Kalispell 59901
Overland, G. M...............1547 S. Higgins, Missoula 59801

Pacheco, Theodore F..............209 W. 2nd St., Libby 59923
Packwood, Burley T.........17th W. & Ave. D, Billings 59102
R Packwood, Palmer......................Box 419, Red Lodge 59068
Pellett, William R.....................11 S. 7th, Miles City 59301
Peters, John R...204 Mayer Bldg., 129 W. Park, Butte 59701
Petersen, John S..................520 2nd St., Whitefish 59937
Peterson, Donald E....17th St. W. & Ave. D, Billings 59102
Peterson, Ivan J., Jr...........301 5th St. S.W., Sidney 59270
Peterson, Wyman C.............20 9th St. E., Kalispell 59901
Petterson, Leroy M.............210 Filicetti Bldg., Havre 59501
Phelps, Garr T...................513 Main St., Deer Lodge 59722
Power, Francis C.............1530 24th St. W., Billings 59101
Prill, Richard D...................823 N. 29th St., Billings 59101

Quinn, James A..................330 Fuller Ave., Helena 59601
Quinn, V. J.............301-3 Miner's Bank Bldg., Butte 59701

Rader, William A.........Box 746, 328 3rd St., Havre 59501
Radley, Penrose H...............907 Helena Ave., Helena 59601
R Rafish, Samuel M.............414 W. Granite Dr., Butte 59701
Raye, Stanley C............802 22nd St. S., Great Falls 59401
Raykowski, Harley A., Jr.....717 W. Central, Missoula 59801
Rector, Robert W...................122 3rd Ave., Havre 59501
Redenius, Myron E.....331 Hart-Albin Bldg., Billings 59101
Reineke, F. G.....................515 Kensington, Missoula 59801
Renouard, C. S.....304-305 Miners Bank Bldg., Butte 59701
Reynolds, F. Gordon...........131 S. Higgins, Missoula 59801
Reynolds, Marvin P.........204 Wilma Bldg., Missoula 59801
Rider, T. T..............................210 N. Higgins, Missoula 59801
Ritter, Richard C...............300 N. Willson, Bozeman 59715
Roberts, Milo C......................................Rt. 4, Kalispell 59901
Roch, Harry Z.............3920 3rd Ave. S., Great Falls 59401

Roche, John D.....Box 995, 795 Sunset Blvd., Kalispell 59901
Roche, Richard A.........406 Metals Bank Bldg., Butte 59701
Romers, Robert D..............................Box 792, Dillon 59725
Romers, William D..............⁚.208 Mayer Bldg., Butte 59701
Romers, William J....................2910 Moulton, Butte 59701
Rowling, Gordon James............10 S. Idaho St., Butte 59701

Sandquist, Donald D...........1224 W. Main, Hamilton 59840
Sanford, A. R........................415 4th St. S.E., Sidney 59270
Schneider, Lawrence L............Capitol Hill Shopping Center,
Helena 59601
Schroeder, R. W..........218 Central Ave., Whitefish 59937
Schultz, Peter J.........2515 6th Ave. S., Great Falls 59401
Schuyler, George L...Ave. D. & 17th St. W., Billings 59102
Schwin, Fred R.....................P. O. Box 97, Red Lodge 59068
Searl, Frank V.....P. O. Box 1528, 328 3rd St., Havre 59501
Shaver, Dean S....................939 Grand Ave., Billings 59102
Shaver, J. M.............503 Montana Bldg., Lewistown 59457
R Shaver, R. C............................3001 Briggs, Missoula 59801
Sherer, Frederick L.....1125 2nd Ave. N., Great Falls 59401
Sherman, R. M.........................P. O. Box 669, Libby 59923
Sherry, Evan T......................P. O. Box 581, Havre 59501
Silva, James D.............................10 S. Idaho, Butte 59701
Slade, Mac L.............1711 13th St. W., Billings 59102
Small, John Milton....201 Montana Bldg., Great Falls 59401
Small, Kenneth C.........3511 1st Ave. N., Great Falls 59401
Smith, George W....109 Riverview 7 W., Great Falls 59401
Smith, James E...................P. O. Box 654, Livingston 59047
Smith, John H...................15 Montana Ave., Laurel 59044
Smollack, Stephen W.........300 Hickory St., Anaconda 59711
R Snow, H. G...............1107 W. Geyser St., Livingston 59047
Solem, B. L...............323 Hart-Albin Bldg., Billings 59101
Spurgin, Charles D............210 Hauser Blvd., Helena 59601
Squire, Donald M..............218 E. Front St., Missoula 59801
Steffensen, Kenneth R........304 Grand Ave., Billings 59102
Stephens, C. E...........302 Strain Bldg., Great Falls 59401
Stoddard, Alice M.................................P. O. Box 577,
White Sulphur Springs 59645
Stout, Fred J.................628 South Ave. W., Missoula 59801
Stroeher, James S....205-6 Hart-Albin Bldg., Billings 59101
Sullivan, Dean P., Sr...............307-8 Treasure State Bldg.,
Billings 59101
Sullivan, James J.............2818 9th Ave. N., Billings 59101
Swanson, C. H., Sr...Columbus 59019

Towney, David B., Jr.........1547 S. Higgins, Missoula 59801
R Taylor, D. S.............................710 S. 3rd, Hamilton 59840
Taylor, Robert N...............406 Electric Bldg., Billings 59101
Terrill, A. Jack...............1927 Jerome Pl., Helena 59601
Thiegs, Richard T.......P. O. Box 308, Thompson Falls 59873
Thomas, William G.........1711 13th St. W., Billings 59102
Thomas, Charles S...............Montana Bldg., Lewistown 59457
Thompson, Albert J............1231 N. 29th St., Billings 59101
Thompson, John N.............P. O. Box 400, Wolf Point 59201
Thompson, Wayne E.......................414 1st Natl. Bldg.,
Bozeman 59715
Tiddy, William R....402 1st Natl. Bank Bldg., Helena 59601
R Towey, Thomas......................P. O. Box 846, Conrad 59425
Tursich, Thomas S.....204 North 11th Ave., Bozeman 59715

Valacich, Walter B.......College Park Medical-Dental Center,
Great Falls 59401

Vallie, Floyd W...........College Park Medical-Dental Center, Great Falls 59401

Wade, William L., Jr...............235 E. Pine, Missoula 59801
Weber, Richard A................P. O. Box 888, Glasgow 59230
Welty, Willis A............P. O. Box 1018, Fort Benton 59442
Westlake, Gordon...............P. O. Box 188, Bozeman 59715
Westler, George D.........1020 1st Ave. S., Great Falls 59401
Weyer, E. S...........................2312 Pine St., Billings 59101
Wheeler, Roger A...............304 Grand Ave., Billings 59102
White, John M.....Medical-Dental Center, Miles City 59301
White, Lester A. L.............445 3rd Ave. E., Kalispell 59901
White, Lonny H. ....17th St. W. & Ave. D., Billings 59102

Whitsell, Frederick L........2210 Brooks St., Missoula 59801
Wilhelm, Paul J.......306 Montana Bldg., Great Falls 59401
Winegardner, Kenneth R...173 LaSalle Road, Kalispell 59901
Wisner, Byron R...1231 N. 29th St., Rm. 309, Bilings 59101
Wolfe, Deloit R.....................129 W. Kent, Missoula 59801
Wood, Douglas E........................Box 1084, 940 1st Ave. E., Kalispell 59901

Yunck, Harry R..................P. O. Box 1117, Conrad 59425

Zimmerman, Lloyd L.................305 Medical-Dental Center, Missoula 59801
Ziolkowski, Harold W...623 N.E. Main St., Lewistown 59457

OUT-OF-STATE DENTISTS

As of September 1, 1970

Alderman, Samuel I...........................6226 W. Manchester Ave., Los ·Angeles, Calif. 90045

Anderson, Gerald D.........723 E. 1st St., Meridian, Idaho 83642

Austin, Cyrus W..............968 Circle Dr., Corvallis, Ore. 97330

Baker, LCDR (DC) Terrance W...........H.S.S. Simon Lake As-33, Fleet P. O. N. Y. 09501

Bale, Dennis E.....2114 S. 11th E., Salt Lake City, Utah 84106

Barnard, Steven A............540 4th St., Idaho Falls, Idaho 83401

Bafes, Donald E...................Box 757, Atascadero, Calif. 93422

Baum, Lloyd...............11460 Aster, Loma Linda, Calif. 92354

Beaton, Donald E................811 12th St., Rawlins, Wyo. 82301

Becker, Carryl M..................................1001 S. University Blvd., Denver, Colo. 80209

Beier, Bruce R..................200 E. 4th, Freeman, S. Dak. 57029

Beitey, Gerald J.....................Box 200, Lakeland Village, Medical Lake, Wash. 99022

Belko, Boris B...........10329 Hole Ave., Arlington, Calif. 92505

Berdeaux, Robert H.....1245 Graham Rd., Florissant, Mo. 63031

Beveridge, E. E..........................2010 Wilshire Blvd., Suite 901, Los Angeles, Calif.

Bideganeta, J. F...........Box 523, Mountain Home, Idaho 83647

Bisson, Roger E...362,1 Bonita Glen Terrace, Bonita, Calif. 92002

Bjorndahl, Robert W...3183 N. Lexington, St. Paul, Minn. 55112

Blaisdell, Reed R.........1720 Arlington, Caldwell, Idaho 83605

Blenkner, Robert C.......5150 Yale Circle, Denver, Colo. 80222

Bock, Ernest T.................P. O. Box 845, Tulelake, Calif. 96134

Bangers, Barry M.......712 Center St., Marysville, Kans. 66508

Bongers, Leo V.....Hanover Clinic Bldg., Hanover, Kans. 66945

Bosshardt, Lowell L............................15734 Ashworth Ave. N., Seattle, Wash. 98133

Boyce, William A...........375 3rd St., Idaho Falls, Idaho 83401

Braten, Ray A..................................P. O. Box 220, 150 S. Main, Buffalo, Wyo. 82834

Brinkman, Jack L....,......260 E. 15th Ave., Eugene, Ore. 97401

Brown, Allen W...................................3239 Prince Valient Dr., San Antonio, Tex. 78218

Bruce, Charles P..............100 W. Boston, Chandler, Ariz. 85224

Bruck, Thomas L.......1665 E. Noble Pl., Littleton, Colo. 80120

Bunn, Larry R..............1900 Memorial Dr., Ceres, Calif. 95307

Bussen, James F....................................7104 Chicago Ave. S., Minneapolis, Minn. 55423

Butori, Eugene F......1033 S.W., Yamhill, Portland, Ore. 97205

Carter, James R...213 S. Broadway Ave., Riverton, Wyo. 82501

Carter, Richard L...437 N. Circle Dr., Colorado Springs, Colo. 80909

Chehey, Charles' L...........605 N. Moore, Moscow, Idaho 83843

Christman, Peter D.....92 Medical Det., APO New York 09165

Clawson, J. R..........1202 Huntington Bldg., Miami, Fla. 33131

Colbern, Robert J...............................520 W. 5th St., Suite C, Oxnard, Calif. 93030

Collings, George J...................Box 16248, 316 S.E. 80th Ave., Portland, Ore. 97216

Collins, Charles P.......................................Kemmerer, Wyo. 83101

Coughren, Kenneth D.....2408 Road 76 N., Pasco, Wash. 99301

Covert, Harvey N...1311 Beechwood Rd., Columbus, Ohio 43227

Crellin, James A.....1218 Plantation Blvd., Jackson, Miss. 39211

Cross, Elias G., Jr...3030 N. Hancock, Colorado Springs, Colo. 80907

Cunningham, James B.......Box 446, Rapid City, S. 'Dak. 57701

Daehlin, Douglas R.........311 Penrose, San Angelo, Tex. 76901

D'Angelo, Eugene L...............877 W. Fremont Ave., Suite H-3, Sunnyvale, Calif. 94087

Davis, Leicester N., Jr...110 S. Gould St., Sheridan, Wyo. 82801

Dean, David L.............1115 S. 119th St., Omaha, Neb. 68144

Deatherage, John F..4th & Washington, La Grande, Ore. 97850

Dedan, Lloyd H.......2900 Piedmont Ave., Duluth, Minn. 55811

Delmore, Michael C.....1110 S. 8th St., Manitowac, Wis. 54220

DeMarois, R. E...............170 2nd Ave. E., Chico, Calif. 95926

Doerr, Eugene A,.........................Box 529, Basin, Wyo. 82410

Dolliver, Donald A.....30 Miller Pl., San Francisco, Calif. 94108

Dougherty, James M.....................................7020 Adelphi Rd., Hyattsville, Md. 20782

Doyle, George G......................Rt. No. 1, Catalo, Idaho 83810

Driscoll, Daniel M.......10631 18th S.W., Seattle, Wash. 98146

Eakins, Donald E.....Box 1235, Steamboat Springs, Colo. 80477

Eastep, Victor J...1840 Mt. View Ave., Longmont, Colo. 80501·

Eastwood, Gerald W.....4006 Jeffry St., Wheaton, Md. 20906

Edwards, Talbert P...............113 E. Park Row, Arlington, Tex.

Ehrlich, Fred E....7631 212th St. S.W., Edmonds, Wash. 98020

Erickson, Donald E.............145 N. 2nd St., Dixon, Calif. 95620

Fallon, Walter W...............P. O. Box 669, Basin, Wyo. 82410

Farnsworth, Robert H.......................3413 Ashley Lane, Apt. F, Indianapolis, Ind. 46224

Fiehrer, Daniel R.......2741 Crest Road, Cincinnati, Ohio 45239

Flaiz, Theodore S.........340 N. Claypool, Prineville, Ore. 97754

Fraser, Francis L.......................14810 Lake Hills Blvd., Suite A, Bellevue, Wash. 98004

Fredricks, Robert J..............418 Juniper St., Chico, Calif. 95926

Friedrich, F. J., Jr.............1507 3rd St., Tillamook, Ore. 97141

Gage, Gary L.........307 St. John's Way, Lewiston, Idaho 83501

Galloway, Robert H...361 Main, Box 466, Chadran, Neb. 69337

Gambill, Donald L................105 Garden Valley Medical Center, Roseburg, Ore. 97470

Garrett, David P...........87 S. Main St., Kaysville, Utah 84037

Gau, George M...........214 E. Birch, Walla Walla, Wash. 99362

Gehan, Paul J................Project Concern, Alpine, Tenn. 38549

Gibbens, F. Treacy........142 N. Main, Garrison, N. Dak. 58540

Girolami, John J...230 F. St., Suite A, Chula Vista, Calif. 92010

Gossett, Ray S.................325 W. Main, Riverton, Wyo. 82501

Granger, Donald C..................................8995 W. 32nd Ave., Wheat Ridge, Colo. 80033

Grulke, Duane A..Avoco, Iowa 51521

Hanson, Duane T...................Skylark Shopping Center, Willmar, Minn. 56201

Harken, James H......................................12418 E. Saltese Rd., Opportunity, Wash. 99216

Harrington, Gerald W..............................3914 N.E. 100th St., Seattle, Wash. 98125
Heath, Robert W.......209 Nu State Bldg., Rockford, Ill. 61101
Hegge, George L...........11 E. 4th St., Williston, N. Dak. 58801
Hoffferber, Allen E...22600 S. Crenshaw Blvd., Torrance, Calif.
Hoffman, Cordelia C..........................2421 Pillsbury Ave. S., Minneapolis, Minn. 55404
Hoffman, Kenneth A............................2421 Pillsbury Ave. S., Minneapolis, Minn. 55404
Holm, Ivan E..................37111 Tripoli, Barstow, Calif. 92311
Hunt, Gordon........105 W. 37th Ave. San Mateo, Calif. 94403

Johnson, Harold J..........P. O. Box 335, Cando, N. Dak. 58324
Johnson, Merle W..................................9174 1 St., Box 1075, Hesperia, Calif. 92345
Johnson, Thomas E....18315 98th N.E., Bothell, Wash. 98011
Johnston, Clarence E.........................421 Coeur d'Alene Ave., Coeur d'Alene, Idaho 83814
Jones, Harper L.......207 Hachler Bldg., Pendleton, Ore. 97801
Jones, T. J.....629 Medical-Dental Bldg., Everett, Wash. 98201
Jones, Wayne N.....1535 S. Blvd., Idaho Falls, Idaho 83401
Joyce, Delmar R..............239 F St., Chula Vista, Calif. 92010

Kampfer, Leslie S......................................10845 Lindbrook Dr., Los Angeles, Calif. 90024
Kaylor, David F..100 N. College Ave., College Place, Wash. 99324
Keilman, Leo A.........800 W. 18th St., The Dalles, Ore. 97058
Kelly, Joseph C......6226 Spring St., Long Beach, Calif. 90815
Kennedy, W. J.........3430 Forest Ave., San Jose, Calif. 95117
Killip, D. E.................University of Iowa, College of Dentistry, Iowa City, Iowa 52240
Killoy, William J..........................48th TAC Hospital, Box 4056, APO New York 09179
King, David J.............4950 Gratiot Rd., Saginaw, Mich. 48603
Kjos, Lloyd A...........202 1st Ave. Bldg., Minot, N. Dak. 58701
Knodle, Jack M...................................5917 Meadowbrook Lane, Lincoln, Neb. 68510
Kortsch, William E............................3204 N. Cambridge Ave., Milwaukee, Wis. 53211
Krusee, Maj. Paul A..................2941 S. Bomarc, Tyndall AFB, Florida 32401

Lamey, David M...705 Med.-Dent. Bldg., Everett, Wash. 98201
Lebsack, Edwin W...................................5th & St. Joseph Ave., Hastings, Neb. 68901
Lewark, Norman L..............:........3041 S. Bellaire St., Denver, Colo.
Lofstrand, James E............10855 N. Wolfe Rd., Vallco Village, Cupertino, Calif. 95014
Lund, Leo N...................17 Hout Bldg., Corvallis, Ore. 97330
Lundberg, B. L........................Box 660, Golden, B. C., Canada
Lyman, Denis R........................Box 126, Jackson, Wyo. 83001

Macho, Albert F.....1616 N.E. 15th Ave., Portland, Ore. 97232
Madden, John P.........Rt. 1, Box 44, Moxee City, Wash. 98936
Magnuson, Ronald E.....2007 Jackson St., Golden, Colo. 80401
Maixner, Frank W..............1224 N. 5th, Seward, Neb. 68434
Malmin, Oscar..............127 E. Wayne Ave., Akron, Ohio 44301
Marmon, Jack S...................Box 2 FPO, Seattle, Wash. 98790
Mayerle, Ronald A............257 Windsor, Medford, Ore. 97501
McChesney, W. R.....4965 W. Hillside Dr., Eugene, Ore. 97405
McCune, Robert J...40 Graceland Dr., San Rafael, Calif. 94901

McIntosh, James J..4966 Glenway Ave., Cincinnati, Ohio 45238
Meany, John J...........1924 Almond St., Anaheim, Calif. 92805
Meese, Robert A.............710 N. Alvernon, Tucson, Ariz. 85711
Mercer, Robert D.....2722 N.E. 33rd Ave., Portland, Ore. 97212
Milanovich, Phillip J.........420 N. Pine St., Chicago, Ill. 60644
Miller, Arthur S......240 S. Quince St., Philadelphia, Pa. 19107
Mohr, Lee J...7280 Irving St., No. 4, Westminster, Colo. 80030
Monson, Melvin V............3427 Lakeside Apts., Iowa City, Iowa
Moore, Jack Lowell....Dept. of Pedodontics, School of Dentistry, U. of Maryland, Baltimore, Md.
Moore, Kathryn A.......Dept. of Pedodontics, School of Dentistry, U. of Maryland, Baltimore, Md.
Moore, Roy A.........201 San Juan Ave., Alamosa, Colo. 81101
Moore, Thomas P...............................420 N.E. Ravenna Blvd., Seattle, Wash. 98115
Moran, J. R...............E. 10909 Boone, Spokane, Wash. 99206
Morris, H. William....................Box 160, Plummer, Idaho 83851
Marstad, Andrew T....Rt. 1, Box 361, Forest Lake, Minn. 55025
Mulick, Edward J.............4129 Bong Rd., Lincoln, Neb. 68524
Murphy, J. G........6509 N.E. 181st St., Seattle, Wash. 98155
Myers, John A..............1096 S. Dora St., Ukiah, Calif. 95482

Nasi, John H..............Box 482, Mt. Edgecumbe, Alaska 99835
Naughton, Richard T..................................406 N.E. 120th Ave., Portland, Ore. 97220
Noel, Lloyd E., Jr............612 1st Ave., Coronado, Calif. 92118

O'Brien, William E...882 Boysen Ave., San Luis Obispo, Calif. 93401
Ogrin, Rodney F.......................................Valley Medical Center, Santa Barbara, Calif. 93105
Omlid, L. E.....806 Med. Arts Bldg., Minneapolis, Minn. 55402
Ostlind, Kenneth D.......843 S Center St., Casper, Wyo. 82601

Packer, Merrill W...........680 Beth Lane, Lexington, Ky. 40503
Peach, Roy N.....................211 W. 9th, Casper, Wyo. 82601
Post, Arthur C....U. S. Army Tripler Gen. Hosp., Tripler Army Med. Center, APO San Francisco 96438
Powell, Murray R.......1120 Francis St., Longmont, Colo. 80501
Pressman, Harold A.................................1496 Windemere Dr., Minneapolis, Minn. 55421

Reid, Fran D.........415 Washington St., The Dalles, Ore. 97058
Rennie, E. G..University Park, Iowa
Richter, William A...........................1663 S.W. Westwood Dr., Portland, Ore. 97201
Robocker, Robert E...........1240 High St., Auburn, Calif. 95603
Rowe, Nathaniel H...................................2107 Devonshire Rd., Ann Arbor, Mich. 48104

Savage, Terry R.......101 W. Naches Ave., Selah, Wash. 98942
Schilke, Lester S...........913 W. Lewis St., Pasca, Wash. 99301
Schlieman, David R.....441 5th St. W., Sonoma, Calif. 95476
Scott, E. M.......................240 W. Osborn, Phoenix, Ariz. 85013
Shannon, James V...........2 Brewster Circle, Hingham, Mass.
Shupe, Robert V........................Box 356, Oroville, Wash. 98844
Siess, Herbert W.........................P. O. Box 348, 320 Solano, Corning, Calif. 96021
Smidt, Donald R...................................1702 Pat Booker Rd., Universal City, Tex. 78148

Smith, Douglas C.................Denver General Hospital, West 6th
    Ave. & Cherokee St., Denver, Colo. 80204
Smith, Don H.....................610 Elm St., Pullman, Wash. 99163
Smith, Sydney M.................520 W. 6th St., Reno, Nev. 89503
Smith, W. M...........930.1 B, California Ave., South Gate, Calif.
Smale, H. Douglas....USPHS Hospital, Red Lake, Minn. 90280
Snurr, N. Glenn......116 W. Main St., Waynesboro, Pa. 17268
Snyder, John R.....103 Cossitt No. 103, La Grange, Ill. 60525
Sorenson, James A.....938 Dewing Ave., LaFayette, Calif. 94549
Sorte, Curtis B...............936 W. 8th Ave., Albany, Ore. 97321
Sowle, Stuart O...........1216 Talcott Bldg., Rockford, Ill. 61101
Steinhauer, Peter F.....1120 Alpine Ave., Boulder, Colo. 80302
Stephens, Paul H...............1184 Olive St., Eugene, Ore. 97401
Stevens, Mark M........U. S. Navy Dent. Clinic, Treasure Island,
    San Francisco, Calif.
Stevens, Otto O.....................W. 2603 Wellesley Ave.,
    Spokane, Wash. 99205
Stackhouse, Burton E...325 W. Main St., Riverton, Wyo. 82501
Stokan, Edward F., Jr...80 Arch St., Redwood City, Calif. 94062
Stowell, Richard K...12755 S.W. 2nd St., Beaverton, Ore. 97005
Sullivan, Dean P, Jr................156 Emerson Ave. E.,
    West St. Paul, Minn. 55118
Sullivan, E. T.....41 W. McCreight Ave., Springfield, Ohio 45504

Tadvick, Thomas G...........................600 Center Ave.,
    Grand Junction, Colo. 81501
Taylor, John S.....................3980 San Pablo Dam Rd.,
    El Sobrante, Calif. 94803
Temple, William R....................Colfax Medical-Dental Bldg.,
    Colfax, Wash. 99111
Terkla, Louis G...1215 S.W. Lancaster St., Portland, Ore. 97219
Thompson, Robert T...................................1110 Lowry Ave. N.,
    Minneapolis, Minn. 55411
Thompson, Wayne D.....Linda Terrace, Apt. 1, 135 Nova Albion
    Way, San Rafael, Calif. 94903

Tipps, James O...Cheney, Kans. 67025
Tromly, Maj. Robert R.....................................71 Delafield Dr.,
    Fort Leonard Wood, Mo. 65473
Turner, Maj. Donald C................603 Cherry, Vandenberg AFB,
    Calif. 93437

Ver Helst, James A...141 W. 20th, Farmington, N. Mex. 87401
Vickernam, William A......................16511 Goldenwest,
    Huntington Beach, Calif. 94646

Wakefield, Leslie A.........2009 Main St., Florence, Ariz. 85232
Weber, Eugene R..............................1515 W. Wisconsin Ave,
    Appleton, Wis. 54911
Weinberg, Jacob E.........Monell, Chem Senses Lab, U. of Penn.,
    Philadelphia, Pa. 19104
Wessels, Wyman E.......625 Broadway, San Diego, Calif. 92101
Wiggins, E. Thomas...........1050 Eldorado, Trail, B. C. Canada
Williams, S. B.......................Box 190, Cardston, Alta., Canada
Williamson, Walter E. L.......................1617 S. Brentwood Blvd.,
    St. Louis, Mo. 63144
Willis, Leon M......................................303 S. Circle Dr.,
    Colorado Springs, Colo. 80909
Wilson, Gary T.....760 Washburn, Suite 4, Corona, Calif. 91720
Wilson, William R...........1541 E. Clark, Pocatello, Idaho 83201
Winters, Dean G...........136 N. Carbon Ave., Price, Utah 84501
Wiprud, C. W...............410 S. Fulton St., Albany, Ore. 97321
Wolgamot, Thomas C.....................................5219 A. Montague,
    Ft. Bliss, Tex. 79906

Young, Harold E..........................111 Plaza Professional Bldg.,
    El Cerrito, Calif. 94530

Zimmerman, Buford H.....................................9406 E. Sprague,
    Spokane, Wash. 99206

DENTAL HYGIENISTS

As of September 1, 1970

Anderson, Natalie V............................Box 546, Helena 59601

Borgmeyer, Janis Lee........3105 Old Pond Rd., Missoula 59801
Bateman, Karen M.........1608 Judson, Richland, Wash. 99352
Bateman, Sally L..............918 Welch Blvd., Flint, Mich. 48504
Betts, Diana...........................245 N. Ave. W., Missoula 59801
Biegel, Joyce L...........................2024 Ave. C, Billings 59102
Buchanan, Jeannette S............Box 220, Columbia Falls 59912
Buer, Lorrayne R..............4000 4th Ave. S., Great Falls 59401
Burch, Joyce A.......305 Thistleton Circle, Lexington, Ky. 40502

Cahill, Mary J..........1136 W. Quince, Olympia, Wash. 98501
Cherry, Mary S...................P. O. Box 208, Fort Benton 59442
Collins, Celine A............W. 803 18th, Spokane, Wash. 99203
Collins, Sandra..........................1417 Fox St., Bozeman 59715
Conver, Nancy K...2209 S. 23rd E., Salt Lake City, Utah 84109
Corrick, Barbara...................115 Takima Dr., Missoula 59801
Cory, Helen C.................504½ Central W., Great Falls 59401
Creon, Jacqueline A........................Box 155, Whitefish 59937

Dalich, Mildred..............2716 6th Ave. N., Great Falls 59401

Erickson, Edna J...................1231 N. 29th St., Billings 59101

Flaherty, Benita L................428 Parkway Dr., Kalispell 59901
Ford, Tessie C.............6 22nd St. N.W., Great Falls 59401
Frahm, Audrey L....4017 51st St. S.W., Seattle, Wash. 98116
Fraser, Beatrice H.............1112 8th Ave. N., Great Falls 59401

Gear, Margaret L.............................14 Ave. B, Billings 59101
Gehan, Jeanne B............Project Concern, Alpine, Tenn. 38543
Golay, Sandra.........Rt. No. 1, Box 266, Hansen, Idaho 93334
Grosso, Marilyn L.......2215 S.E. Salmon, Portland, Ore. 97214

Haas, Cathryn...................Box 526, Wahpeton, N. Dak. 58075
Hofer, Ann N..............1932 Beverly Hills Blvd., Billings 59102
Hakert, Bonnie...............1048 N. 28th St., Billings 59101
Hall, Margaret M.................................Box 8, Harrison 59735
Halterman, Gwendolyn V................................1247 14th Ave.,
San Francisco, Calif. 94122
Hanna, Joan T.................1711 13th St. W., Billings 59102
Hansford, Carol J............425 Laurel Ave., Plentywood 59254
Henningsen, Patricia.......................3115 Sheridan, Butte 59701
Herman, Jerralyn.........................7246 E. Park Way, Apt. 1,
Sacramento, Calif. 95823
Hungerford, Carol......................25 Corinthian Court, No. 32,
Tiburon, Calif. 94920

LeKander, Gloria J.........127 15th Ave., Lewiston, Idaho 93501

Lichtwardt, Shirley B..............................6907 Cherrywood Dr.,
Colorado Springs, Colo. 80907
Long, Lorna B.....3818 Barbara Ave., Bakersfield, Calif. 93309

Mangnall, Marilyn C..............634 3rd Ave. S., Glasgow 59230
Marmon, Donna E................Box 2 FPO, Seattle, Wash. 98790
Martin, Nancy N.......PHS Indian Health, Box Elder 59521
Mayerle, Patricia J..........257 Windsor, Medford, Ore. 97501
McKellar, Gayle A...................523 E. Central, Missoula 59801
Mills, Patricia F................................Rimini Rt., Helena 59601
Minnehan, Patricia..................................Box 73, Joplin 59531
Mohr, Sharon C...375 S. Depeu, Apt. 103, Denver, Colo. 80226
Moriarty, Doris J.....310 S. 1st St., Council Bluffs, Iowa 51501

Ness, Jean M..................228 N. Poplar St., Plentywood 59254
Nockleby, Kathryn K..1210 3rd St. S.,
Moorhead, Minn. 56560

Oakland, Sharon D.............3609 1st Ave. S., Great Falls 59401
Oberg, Ann..................2610 "A" Almeda, Norfolk, Va. 23513
Opitz, Eleanor S..........10211 23rd N.E., Seattle, Wash. 98125

Pellett, Barbara G............................11 S. 7th, Miles City 59301
Peterson, Helen M..........17th St. W. & Ave. D, Billings 59102
Pinney, Betty J...................1839 West Central, Missoula 59801
Poirot, Barbara K..................1050 Yreka Ct., Missoula 59801

Reiersgaard, Mary K..........713 46th St. S., Great Falls 59401
Rodolph, Mary Kay...............Box 112, Clovis, N. Mex. 88101
Rowling, Diane L.......10 S. Idaho St., Room 304, Butte 59701

Smart, Estelle..................305 80th St., Brooklyn, N. Y. 11209
Snyder, Eunice....103 E. Cossitt, No. 103, La Grange, Ill. 60525
Stalcup, Catherine D............................615 ACW Sq., Box 284,
APO New York 90409
Sullivan, Diane H..............102 Whitaker Dr., Missoula 59801
Super, Marcia M...................522 N. 5th Ave., Bozeman 59715

Tan, Violeta...........4420 S. Brandon St., Seattle, Wash. 98118
Thomas, Janet M..................1711 13th St. W., Billings 59102
Topel, Irene.....................3912 Lincoln Rd., Missoula 59801

White, Sandra L.................5019 A, Ave. C, Great Falls 59401
Wildgen, Jacqueline....Buffalo Hill Rd., Rt. 3, Kalispell 59901
Williams, Mary Lou..........Box 701, Cottage Grove, Ore. 97424
Wilson, Marcia M.........................25246 Barton Rd., No. 12,
Loma Linda, Calif. 92354
Wiprud, Mary A.............410 S. Fulton St., Albany, Ore. 97321
Wolfe, Maxey L.................E. 1621 36th Ave., Spokane, Wash.